NATIONAL GEOGRAPHIC

Ladders

Common Core Readers

AMAZING PLANTS

AFTER THE WEDDING, PADMA GOT USED TO LIFE AT THE PALACE. SHE AND THE KING WERE THE HAPPIEST COUPLE IN ALL THE LAND.

DREADED WITCH DISLIKED THIER JOY. SHE BEGAN WORKING HARD TO RUIN PADMA'S HAPPINESS.

OUCH!

YOUR JOY WILL NOT LAST. YOUR KING THINKS YOU ARE LESS BEAUTIFUL THAN YESTERDAY!

PADMA MADE A PLAN TO DEFEAT DREADED WITCH. SHE WAS SAD BECAUSE SHE KNEW SHE WOULD HAVE TO GIVE UP HER LIFE WITH THE KING.

PADMA LEFT HER ROOM IN THE MIDDLE OF THE NIGHT.

SHE SNEAKED OUT TO THE PEACEFUL WATER GARDEN BEHIND THE PALACE.

PADMA JUMPED INTO THE POOL IN THE GARDEN. SHE CHANGED INTO A LOTUS FLOWER.

THE KING AWOKE IN THE MORNING. HE HAD A FEELING THAT SOMETHING WAS WRONG. HE DECIDED TO FIND PADMA.

THE KING AND HIS PEOPLE SEARCHED THE PALACE AND ITS GROUNDS, BUT THEY COULD NOT FIND PADMA.

THE KING HAD ALMOST GIVEN UP. THEN HE WALKED TO THE WATER GARDEN. THERE HE SAW THE LOTUS FLOWER IN ITS WATERY **HABITAT**.

WHERE DID THIS BEAUTIFUL FLOWER COME FROM? IT BRINGS ME JOY, AS IF I WERE SEEING PADMA HERSELF.

I MUST DESTROY THAT UGLY FLOWER!

DREADED WITCH CAST A SPELL AND THE WATER DRAINED FROM THE POOL.

THEN SHE CAST ANOTHER SPELL AND THE LOTUS FLOWER BURST INTO FLAMES. ONLY ASHES WERE LEFT.

LATER THAT NIGHT . . .

A TINY PLANT GREW FROM THE ASHES.

IT GREW TALLER AND TALLER.

FROM THE LOTUS ASHES GREW THE FIRST MANGO TREE. IT WAS **BLOOMING** WITH HUNDREDS OF FLOWERS.

YESTERDAY, THIS POOL WAS FULL OF WATER. IN THE POOL BLOOMED ONE BEAUTIFUL LOTUS FLOWER.

IN THIS CHANGED HABITAT THERE IS A TREE I'VE NEVER SEEN. YET ITS **ADAPTATIONS** MAKE IT PERFECT FOR THIS PLACE.

AND IT HAS HUNDREDS OF FLOWERS!

ONE DAY THE KING VISITED THE MANGO TREE. HE SAW FRUIT GROWING FROM ITS BRANCHES.

Check In   What plants did Padma change into?

| **Read to find out** about some of Earth's most extreme plants.

Extreme Plants

by Jennifer Boudart

Plants live in almost every kind of **habitat** on Earth. They grow in ponds and on mountains. Plants even grow in extreme habitats that are very hot, cold, or dry. Plants have **adaptations** that help them live in their habitat. The way plants look and grow helps them live. Some plants have extreme adaptations.

The Biggest Bloomer!

The rafflesia is a plant from Southeast Asia. It grows just one flower. But it's huge. This flower grows up to 1 meter (about 3 feet) across. The **bloom** smells like rotten meat! Flies like the smell. The flies pick up pollen as they crawl on the flower. Then they spread the pollen to other blooms. This is how more of the plants can grow.

The rafflesia's bloom is the largest in the world.

A Green Giant!

The giant sequoia is a giant tree. It has the most mass, or bulk, of any plant. So it is the biggest plant **species.** Its trunk can be more than 6 meters (20 feet) across. Giant sequoias are tall, too. Many are 76 meters (about 250 feet) tall. A few are more than 93 meters (305 feet)!

To see the giant sequoias, you have to visit the Sierra Nevada in eastern California.

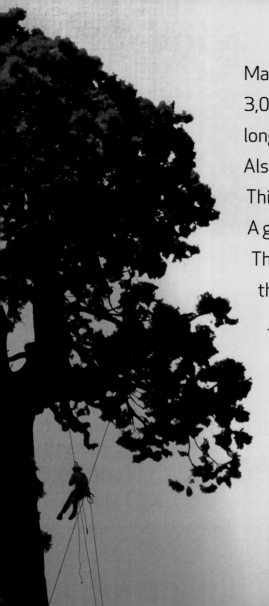

Many giant sequoias have lived more than 3,000 years. What adaptations help them live so long? Their bark protects the tree from disease. Also, giant sequoias can grow new bark quickly. This new bark covers burns from forest fires. A giant sequoia usually dies because it falls over. This happens when the soil can no longer hold the tree's roots.

The General Sherman Tree is the most massive giant sequoia. It is about 84 meters (275 feet) tall. Its trunk is 11 meters (35 feet) wide! Its wood could be used to build 40 houses. But it is against the law to cut down giant sequoias. That's good news for the General Sherman.

Statue of Liberty	General Sherman	U.S. Capitol building
93 meters (305 feet)	84 meters (275 feet)	88 meters (288 feet)

This is King Clone, the oldest known creosote bush. It forms a ring about 14 meters (45 feet) across. Scientists think King Clone first sprouted from a seed 13,700 years ago!

Blast from the Past!

The creosote bush is a desert plant. It grows in the shape of a ring. It is one of the longest-living plants on Earth.

The bush starts out as one parent plant. It can live 200 years. The parent plant sends out shoots all around it. Each shoot grows into a new bush. These bushes are copies of the parent plant. They grow in

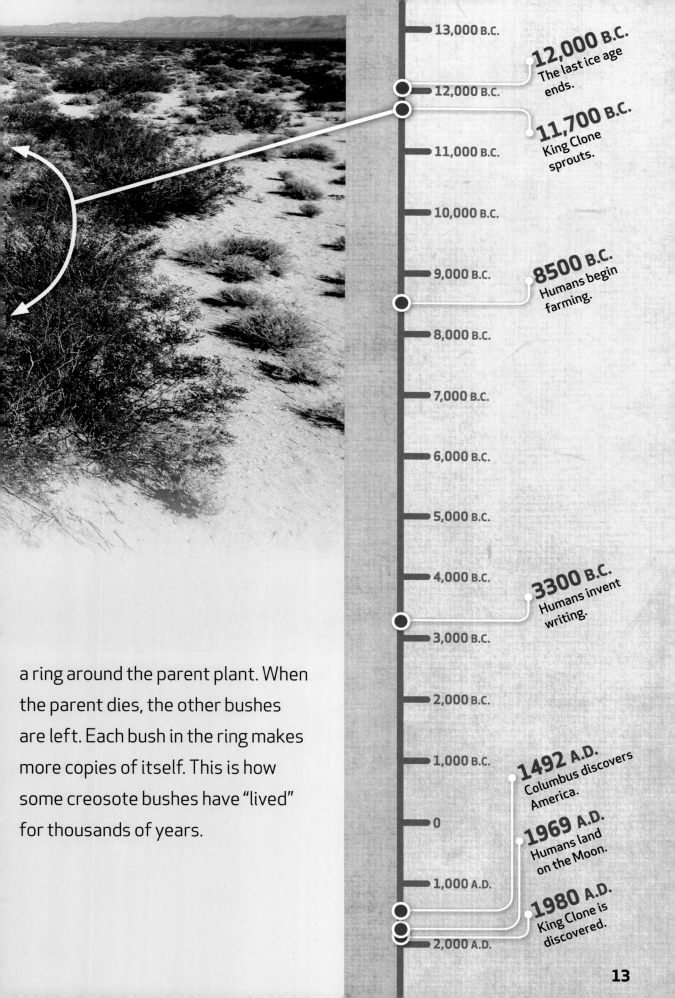

a ring around the parent plant. When the parent dies, the other bushes are left. Each bush in the ring makes more copies of itself. This is how some creosote bushes have "lived" for thousands of years.

13,000 B.C.

12,000 B.C.
The last ice age ends.

12,000 B.C.

11,700 B.C.
King Clone sprouts.

11,000 B.C.

10,000 B.C.

9,000 B.C.

8500 B.C.
Humans begin farming.

8,000 B.C.

7,000 B.C.

6,000 B.C.

5,000 B.C.

4,000 B.C.

3300 B.C.
Humans invent writing.

3,000 B.C.

2,000 B.C.

1,000 B.C.

1492 A.D.
Columbus discovers America.

0

1969 A.D.
Humans land on the Moon.

1,000 A.D.

1980 A.D.
King Clone is discovered.

2,000 A.D.

A Turbo Grower!

Bamboo grows well in East and Southeast Asia. It is wet and warm there. Some species of bamboo may be the fastest-growing plants on Earth.

Bamboos are grasses that look like trees. They have a woody stem and leafy branches. Some species of bamboo grow very tall. Bamboo may also grow very quickly. Some may grow 2.5 centimeters (1 inch) per hour. Imagine if all grasses grew that fast!

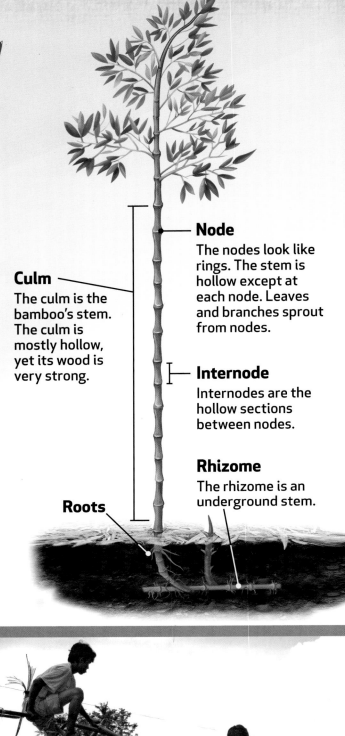

Node
The nodes look like rings. The stem is hollow except at each node. Leaves and branches sprout from nodes.

Culm
The culm is the bamboo's stem. The culm is mostly hollow, yet its wood is very strong.

Internode
Internodes are the hollow sections between nodes.

Rhizome
The rhizome is an underground stem.

Roots

People use bamboo in thousands of ways. The seeds and shoots can be eaten. Its sturdy wood can be used to make furniture, musical instruments, and homes. How are these people using bamboo?

A bamboo forest near Kyoto, Japan

A Microgreen!

Watermeal is the smallest flowering plant species. This tiny, round plant floats. One plant is the size of a small grain of sand. Twelve blooms could fit on the head of a pin! Watermeal does not have roots or stems. Its size and shape are adaptations. They help watermeal plants float together.

A person's fingers show how tiny watermeal plants are.

A giant Amazon water lily can easily support 23 kilograms (50 pounds).

A Leaf Beyond Belief!

Have a seat on a giant Amazon water lily. You won't sink! This plant's huge leaves stretch 2.5 meters (8 feet) across. This plant's adaptations help it float. The weight of its leaves is spread out. Veins in its leaves are filled with air. And notches on the leaves help water drain. This makes sure the leaf doesn't fill and sink.

This giant Amazon water lily can hold three people.

You just read about some plant species with extreme adaptations. Do any extreme plants grow where you live?

Check In Which extreme plants can live for longer than 3,000 years?

The Plant Hunt

by Renee Biermann
illustrated by C. B. Canga

NARRATOR

MRS. BLANKENSHIP
female teacher

INTRODUCTION

[SETTING *The play takes place at City Botanical Gardens. NARRATOR enters and speaks to the audience.*]

NARRATOR: Welcome to City Botanical Gardens! Mrs. Blankenship has brought a special group of students to this indoor **habitat** for a scavenger hunt. She has given them a Scavenger Hunt Notebook, a measuring tape, and gardening gloves. They are going to hunt for five unusual plants. How will they locate these mysterious plants? And what will they discover at the end of the hunt? Let's find out!

MADDIE
female plant hunter

PIPPA
female plant hunter

NOAH
male plant hunter

JIN
male plant hunter

ANTWON
male plant hunter

ANNABELLE
female plant hunter

ACT 1, SCENE 1

[**SETTING** *Near the entrance of City Botanical Gardens.* MADDIE, JIN, ANTWON, NOAH, PIPPA, *and* ANNABELLE *are listening to* MRS. BLANKENSHIP.]

MRS. BLANKENSHIP: Look carefully at your Scavenger Hunt Notebook. Use it as much as possible. Be sure to wear your gardening gloves because some plants are poisonous. Have fun! I'll see you at the end for a *big surprise!*

[*MRS. BLANKENSHIP exits. Students look excited about the big surprise.*]

NOAH: [*holds up Scavenger Hunt Notebook*] Let's look at the notebook together. [*flips through pages and shows group*] There is one page for each plant. We have to mark "yes" or "no" for the plant **characteristics.** We also have to list the plant name. There is room for our comments, too.

Plant Characteristics	Yes	No	Comments
Leaves			
Flowers			
Vines			
Scent			

Plant Name: _____

PIPPA: Where do we begin?

ANTWON: [*pulls piece of folded paper out of pocket*] Mrs. Blankenship gave me this piece of paper when we came in. She told me not to look at it until the hunt started. Maybe it will help.

JIN: Will you read it to us?

ANTWON: It says, "I have a trunk. I stand tall. I'm named after one of the biggest animals of all."

ANNABELLE: [*confused*] That sounds like an elephant! [*excited*] Wait! I saw a big plant that had leaves like elephant ears when we came in.

MADDIE: Let's start there!

SCENE 2

[**SETTING** *All students walk to a tall plant in the corner. The plant has large, broad leaves. The leaves look like elephant ears.*]

JIN: You are right, Annabelle. These leaves sure do look like elephant ears! What a strange **adaptation.**

ANNABELLE: [*points to sign next to plant*] I *was* right. The plant's name is elephant ears!

NOAH: I'll write that down in the notebook. [*checks off characteristics while studying plant*] This plant has leaves, but I don't see any flowers.

MADDIE: [*measuring a leaf with measuring tape*] This leaf is 74 centimeters wide. It's 107 centimeters tall. It's huge! Let's write that in the comments section.

JIN: No flowers are **blooming** on this plant. It doesn't have vines or a scent. Check "no" for those characteristics.

PIPPA: We figured out this plant quickly. But where do we go next? Antwon, did Mrs. Blankenship give you any other clues?

ANTWON: [*holds up clue*] No, this is the only one.

ANNABELLE: Look! [*points to bottom of plant*] There is a new piece of paper!

NOAH: [*reads paper aloud*] "I'm tiny as can be. I'm an itty bitty tree!"

MADDIE: Let's go look for the new plant!

SCENE 3

[**SETTING** *Students are walking along the pathway.*]

PIPPA: [*thinking hard*] There are a bunch of trees in
this habitat. Which one is the clue talking about?

JIN: [*points to nearby plant*] That plant over there
looks like a tiny tree.

NOAH: I think you found it! This one is called a
bonsai tree. [*writes name in notebook*]

PIPPA: The sign says this plant comes
from Japan.

MADDIE: That's amazing! It also has small, pink flowers. [*sniffs*] They have a light scent. [*measures plant*] This plant is only 13 centimeters tall.

[NOAH *records characteristics in notebook.*]

ANNABELLE: It really does look like a tiny tree. We should write that in the comments section.

NOAH: [*writing*] No problem!

[JIN *reaches down. He pulls a piece of paper from under the plant's pot.*]

JIN: I found the new clue! "We do not sit on the ground. Look up high and think of *sound*."

[*Students go to search for next plant.*]

SCENE 4

[**SETTING** *Students are looking at plants that are hanging from the ceiling.*]

NOAH: What kind of musical instruments do we know?

JIN: There's the flute, the saxophone, the violin, the guitar…

ANTWON: [*stops to read a plant name*] I found it! It's called angel's trumpet!

ANNABELLE: Those flowers do look kind of like trumpets. They are beautiful.

MADDIE: [*stretches to measure*] Wow—this plant is 2 meters tall! [*sniffs flowers*] The flowers smell great!

PIPPA: Be careful, Maddie. The sign says this plant is poisonous.

JIN: I'm really happy Mrs. Blankenship gave us these gloves!

[*All students nod and agree with* JIN.]

NOAH: I wrote down the information we need. Who has the next clue?

ANNABELLE: [*pulls clue out of middle of plant*] Here it is! It says: "I make many things taste yummy. Look up high where it's sunny."

ANTWON: [*excited*] I know that one right away! It's a vanilla orchid!

PIPPA: [*doubtful*] How do you know that?

ANTWON: My aunt grows orchids. She told me about the vanilla one. It's a huge vine. [*points to distance*] There it is!

[*Students walk to huge vine growing up a post.*]

PIPPA: I'm sorry I didn't believe you, Antwon. This sign says vanilla orchid. It says all of the vanilla in the world comes from these plants. The sign says they're originally from present-day Mexico.

NOAH: I'm going to write that along with our information. [*begins writing*]

MADDIE: [*looks worried*] Oh, no! I'm never going to be able to measure it. It's so high!

JIN: Let's **estimate** the height. I'm sure Mrs. Blankenship will understand. She wouldn't want us to climb up there!

ANNABELLE: I would estimate that it's about 5 meters tall.

[*Students nod in agreement. NOAH records information.*]

PIPPA: [*sniffs and makes a face*] Do you guys smell something? It stinks!

NOAH: [*sniffs orchid*] It's not this plant. This plant has a sweet scent. [*writes information in notebook*] It must be coming from something else.

JIN: [*pulls out piece of paper that is tucked in vine and reads it*] I think the final clue will help us. Listen to this: "Use your nose to find me. I don't smell like other lilies."

ANTWON: Follow that stinky scent!

SCENE 5

[**SETTING** *Students come around a corner.*
MRS. BLANKENSHIP *is standing next to a gigantic plant. She is holding her nose. NARRATOR enters and addresses audience.*]

NARRATOR: The students are almost finished with the Scavenger Hunt. They have recorded important information about each plant they found. Now, they are ready to find the big surprise—and boy, is it BIG!

MRS. BLANKENSHIP: Surprise! You made it!

[*Students make faces at stinky odor.*]

JIN: What is that?

MADDIE: [*quickly measuring*] It's 1.2 meters tall!

[NOAH *records information in the notebook.*]

MRS. BLANKENSHIP: [*laughing*] This plant is called the voodoo lily. It only blooms once a year. When it blooms, it smells like something is rotting! The scent attracts pollinators to help the plant reproduce.

NOAH: [*makes uncomfortable sound*] That's for sure. It smells awful!

ANNABELLE: [*interested*] I don't care that it smells bad. It's amazing! And it sure is a *big surprise.*

[*Students all nod in agreement.*]

MRS. BLANKENSHIP: [*happy*] I hope you had a good time today. You did a great job of identifying all of the plants. Would you like to come here again sometime?

[*Students all say "yes." They cheer.*]

Check In Which plant does vanilla come from?

Discuss | Characters, Stories, and Main Ideas

1. What do you think connects the three pieces that you read in this book? What makes you think that?

2. Choose an illustration in "The King's Tree." What additional information does it give about the characters or the setting?

3. What is the main idea of "Extreme Plants"? Explain how you think each plant's most extreme feature might be useful to it.

4. In "The Plant Hunt," what event usually leads to the start of a new scene?

5. What do you still wonder about plants? What would be some good ways to find more information?